Weird Fact Puzzles

INSECTS

Helene Hovanec and Kate Ritchey

illustrated by Dave Clegg

STERLING

New York / London
www.sterlingpublishing.com/kids

STERLING and the distinctive Sterling logo are registered trademarks of
Sterling Publishing Co., Inc.

10 9 8 7 6 5 4 3 2 1
07/09

Published by Sterling Publishing Co., Inc.
387 Park Avenue South, New York, NY 10016
Puzzles © 2009 by Helene Hovanec
Text © 2009 by Kate Ritchey
Illustrations © 2009 by Dave Clegg
Distributed in Canada by Sterling Publishing
c/o Canadian Manda Group, 165 Dufferin Street
Toronto, Ontario, Canada M6K 3H6
Distributed in the United Kingdom by GMC Distribution Services
Castle Place, 166 High Street, Lewes, East Sussex, England BN7 1XU
Distributed in Australia by Capricorn Link (Australia) Pty. Ltd.
P.O. Box 704, Windsor, NSW 2756, Australia

Sterling ISBN 978-1-4027-4444-0

For information about custom editions, special sales, premium and
corporate purchases, please contact Sterling Special Sales Department
at 800-805-5489 or specialsales@sterlingpublishing.com.

INTRODUCTION

Weird Fact Puzzles: Insects is a "twofer," or a two-for-the-price-of-one book. You're not only learning the coolest things about insects, but you're also flexing your brain muscles as you solve puzzles to find out even more strange insect facts. What a combo!

When we began to research this book we were amazed at the HUGE amount of information about all the tiny insects on planet Earth. For example:

DID YOU KNOW?

- Insects evolved long before dinosaurs, about 408 to 360 million years ago.

- Insects outnumber humans by over a million times.

- Insects like bees, butterflies, and moths pollinate plants that make food for people; without insects, we would starve.

- Many people around the world eat insects. They are high in vitamins, minerals, and energy.

- Insects can see in ultraviolet light. Scientists refer to this color of light as "bee purple."

We hope you enjoy reading and puzzling about the facts we gathered for you.

Kate and Helene

INSECTS, INSECTS, INSECTS

- All insects have six legs. Spiders, centipedes, and worms are not insects.

- Insect bodies are made up of three parts: the head, the thorax, and the abdomen.

- Insects don't have bones. Instead they have external shells called exoskeletons.

- The exoskeletons of insects looks smooth, but are often covered with hair, hooks, scales, or long threads.

- Insects have compound eyes with thousands of lenses, which allow them to see in almost every direction at the same time.

- Insects use their two antennae to smell and to balance themselves (an extra pair of wings helps too).

- Insects taste with special hairs on their feet.

- Some insects can live, even when parts of their bodies are missing, because they have mini-brains in several places in their bodies in addition to the main brain located in their heads.

SPICE IT UP

Below are 17 things that can be used to add flavor to food. Find these words in the grid by looking up, down, and diagonally, both forward and backward. Circle each word as you find it. Then take the **leftover** letters and write them in the blanks below the grid. Go from *left* to *right* and *top* to *bottom* as you copy the leftovers to find a fact about a spice that might prevent insect bites.

ANISE

BASIL

BAY LEAF

BORAGE

CHIVES

DILL

FLAXSEED

LICORICE

MUSTARD

PARSLEY

PEPPERMINT

PIMENTO

RELISH

ROSEMARY

SAGE

SALT

SHALLOT

P	E	A	T	I	M	U	S	T	A	R	D
N	E	C	I	R	O	C	I	L	Y	E	E
D	G	P	G	A	R	F	L	E	R	G	E
O	I	I	P	C	A	T	L	M	A	A	S
L	T	L	I	E	G	S	L	S	M	R	X
I	H	N	L	T	R	K	A	A	E	O	A
S	E	Y	E	A	E	M	N	E	S	B	L
A	A	P	P	M	L	I	I	N	O	S	F
B	E	C	T	S	I	A	S	N	R	W	A
C	H	I	V	E	S	P	E	Y	T	F	R
O	M	Y	O	S	H	A	L	L	O	T	U

Answer:

___ ___ ___ ___ ___   ___ ___ ___ ___ ___ ___

___ ___ ___ ___ ___   ___ ___ ___

___ ___ ___ ___ ___ ___ ___   ___ ___ ___

___ ___ ___ ___   ___ ___ ___ .

Answer on page 60.

ANTS

- There are more ants than any other single species on Earth.

- Some ants can carry things 50 times heavier than they are.

- Ants have weak vision. Scientists think many of them are actually blind.

- Certain species of ant kill their prey by biting, stinging, or stretching and pulling them to death.

- Some ants herd and milk aphids like we herd and milk cows: They keep them confined and then stroke their antennae to make the aphids produce honeydew.

- Biting ants have been used by people to close wounds: Torn skin is held tightly together, and the ant is placed on the wound, mouth first. The ant bites, piercing the skin with its sharp mouth, and then the body of the ant is cut away, leaving only the biting head as a stitch.

- While on the move, army ants form temporary shelters and bridges out of their own bodies! They cluster together and grip each other with their feet.

- Honeypot ants store nectar and honeydew in some of their worker ants, who remain inside the nest. When food is scarce, the bloated storage ants regurgitate the food for other ants!

- Ants sometimes kidnap larvae from other ants' nests to increase their own number of workers.

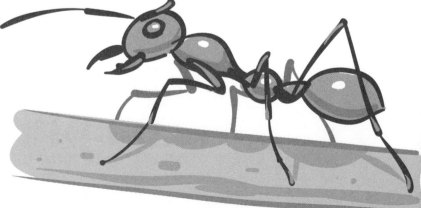

SEW WHAT?

Some insects actually sew groups of leaves together using sticky silk from larvae. To find the names of these insects, take a word from the box below and write it into the blanks on each line to form two new words or phrases. The first word or phrase will end with the word you put on the blanks and the second word or phrase will start with this word. When you're done, copy the letter on each numbered blank to the same-numbered blank at the bottom.

APPLE	BLUE	EVER	HEART	LIGHT
LOVE	NEW	SIDE	TABLE	WOOD

1. FIRE — $\underset{1}{—}$ — — — CHUCK

2. SWEET — $\underset{2}{—}$ — — ACHE

3. PINE $\underset{3}{—}$ — — — — SAUCE

4. PUPPY — — $\underset{4}{—}$ — LETTER

5. NAVY — — — $\underset{5}{—}$ BERRY

6. FOR — — — $\underset{6}{—}$ GREEN

7. COFFEE — $\underset{7}{—}$ — — — CLOTH

8. BRAND $\underset{8}{—}$ — — ENGLAND

9. FLASH — — — — $\underset{9}{—}$ HOUSE

10. OUT $\underset{10}{—}$ — — — WALK

Answer: $\underset{1}{—}\ \underset{2}{—}\ \underset{3}{—}\ \underset{4}{—}\ \underset{5}{—}\ \underset{6}{—}\quad \underset{7}{—}\ \underset{8}{—}\ \underset{9}{—}\ \underset{10}{—}$

Answer on page 64.

BEES

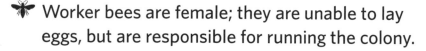

- Medium-sized bumblebees beat their wings about 200 beats per second.

- Bees carry pollen from flowers using brushes and baskets on their legs.

- Honeybees have to collect nectar from about 2 million flowers to make 1 pound (0.5 kilogram) of honey.

- Honeybees can give off a special scent to warn other honeybees of danger.

- Worker bees are female; they are unable to lay eggs, but are responsible for running the colony.

- The female leafcutter bee lays her eggs inside a leaf stem which she cuts open with her jaws.

- Because they can't fly when they're too cold, bumblebees shiver to warm up their muscles before flying in cold weather.

- Bumblebees reach a body temperature of close to 100 degrees Fahrenheit (38 degrees Celsius) when they fly.

- Bees communicate with each other using flight patterns.

- About one-fifth of bees don't raise their own young—they lay eggs in other bees' nests.

- Killer bees are not a natural species. They were created in Brazil in the 1950s when local bees were bred with African honeybees.

BRR!

Fill in the missing letters in the grid to make regular words that make sense when read both *ACROSS* and *DOWN*. Then copy the filled-in letters to the same-numbered spaces below the grid to find out the names of two types of insects that live in Antarctica: one the largest and the other, the most common.

Answer: ___ ___ ___ ___ ___ ___ ___ ___ ___ ___ ___ ___ ___
　　　　　　 1　 2　 3　 4　 5　 6　　7　 8　 9　　10　11　12　13

Answer on page 62.

HOUSING ARRANGEMENTS

Write a letter in each blank to spell a common word. Then read down the center column and write the new word on the line under each hive. Read these words from 1 to 7 to find out how bees dwell.

HU __ A N
GR __ U P
WA __ T E
WA __ C H

1. _____

HO __ B Y
SW __ A T
CH __ S S
ME __ S Y

2. _____

SO __ I D
CR __ S P
SE __ E N
QU __ E N

3. _____

10

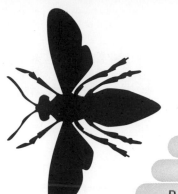

B O __ R D
H E __ L O
C L __ W N
S I __ C E
B R __ A K

4. _____

P U __ C H
S P __ O N
F E __ C H

5. _____

B R __ S K
R A __ C H

6. _____

O C __ U R
S T __ N E
S I __ L Y
C R __ W D
W I __ G S
G R __ M E
B L __ E D
P A __ T E

7. _____

Answer: _____ _____ _____ _____ ,
　　　　　　1　　　　2　　　　3　　　　4

_____ _____ _____ .
　5　　　6　　　　7

Answer on page 60.

BEETLES

- There are over 350,000 different known species of beetle.

- Beetles have four wings: two which form a hard protective casing, and two delicate ones with which they fly.

- Some desert beetles collect water by allowing morning dew to condense on their bodies.

- Some scarab beetles have antennae which open like a fan.

- Fireflies, also known as glow-worms, are actually beetles, not worms. The females can flash their tails, giving off a soft, greenish light. They light up to locate mates.

- The light a firefly gives off is one-fortieth as bright as the light of a candle.

- Fireflies can control their flashing.

- Female fireflies flash their lights about every two seconds.

- Bombardier beetles blast a boiling, foul-smelling spray (up to 212 degrees Fahrenheit or 100 degrees Celsius) at enemies—ouch! This toxin temporarily blinds their enemies, giving the beetles time to run away.

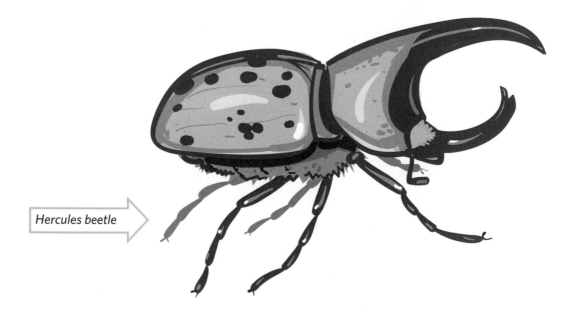

Hercules beetle

EYE SEE YOU

Look at the first word on each line and think of its opposite. Fill it in on the blank spaces to form a new, longer word. Then write the numbered letters on the same-numbered spaces below to find the name of an insect that lives in water and has eyes with two parts—one that looks above the surface of the water and one that looks below.

1. HIM   A N O T __ __ __
                                      2 11 4

2. FIRST   E __ __ __ I C
                             14   13

3. ASK   I N __ __ __ __ I G E N T
                              15

4. LOSE   T __ __ __ K L E
                           1 3

5. SHORT   B E __ __ __ __ I N G S
                            5   9

6. LOW   __ __ __ __ W A Y
                        6 7

7. FIX   __ __ __ __ __ F A S T
                    10

8. HEALTHY   W I N D M __ __ __
                               8

9. WEST   F __ __ __ __ I N G
                     12

Answer: __ __ __ __ __ __ __ __ __
             1 2 3 4 5 6 7 8 9

__ __ __ __ __ __
10 11 12 13 14 15

Answer on page 62.

EVEN MORE BEETLES

- A screech beetle squeaks when it is picked up.

- Click beetles play dead on their backs if threatened. They can flip up to 6 inches (15 centimeters) in the air to right themselves, making a loud click in the process.

- Diving beetles can breathe underwater by carrying air under their wings and in between long hairs on their bodies.

- Goliath beetles have horn-shaped structures on their heads that they use to fight with each other.

- Male stag beetles often fight over territory and females; whichever beetle picks up the other with its huge jaws and flips it over first wins.

- Also known as "pinching bugs," stag beetles can draw blood if they bite you, but they rarely do.

- Toxic oil beetles (or blister beetles) ooze a poison so deadly that 0.001 ounce (0.003 milliliter) is fatal to humans.

Stag beetle

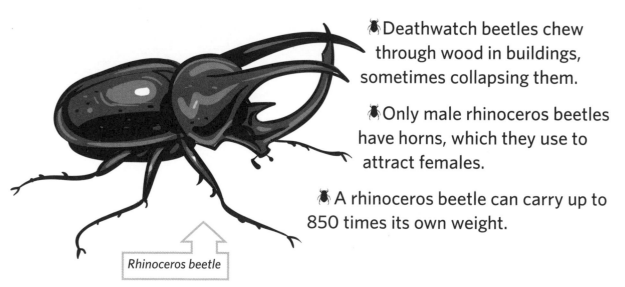

- Deathwatch beetles chew through wood in buildings, sometimes collapsing them.

- Only male rhinoceros beetles have horns, which they use to attract females.

- A rhinoceros beetle can carry up to 850 times its own weight.

Rhinoceros beetle

BIG DEAL

The numbers on a telephone can stand for more than one letter. For example, 2 could be *A*, *B*, or *C*. Choose the correct letter for each number to find a fact about a big insect. The first word has been done for you.

$\underset{8}{\underline{\text{T}}}$ $\underset{4}{\underline{\text{H}}}$ $\underset{3}{\underline{\text{E}}}$ $\underset{4}{\underline{}}$ $\underset{6}{\underline{}}$ $\underset{5}{\underline{}}$ $\underset{4}{\underline{}}$ $\underset{2}{\underline{}}$ $\underset{8}{\underline{}}$ $\underset{4}{\underline{}}$

$\underset{2}{\underline{}}$ $\underset{3}{\underline{}}$ $\underset{3}{\underline{}}$ $\underset{8}{\underline{}}$ $\underset{5}{\underline{}}$ $\underset{3}{\underline{}}$ $\underset{4}{\underline{}}$ $\underset{7}{\underline{}}$

$\underset{8}{\underline{}}$ $\underset{4}{\underline{}}$ $\underset{3}{\underline{}}$ $\underset{4}{\underline{}}$ $\underset{3}{\underline{}}$ $\underset{2}{\underline{}}$ $\underset{8}{\underline{}}$ $\underset{4}{\underline{}}$ $\underset{3}{\underline{}}$ $\underset{7}{\underline{}}$ $\underset{8}{\underline{}}$

$\underset{4}{\underline{}}$ $\underset{6}{\underline{}}$ $\underset{7}{\underline{}}$ $\underset{3}{\underline{}}$ $\underset{2}{\underline{}}$ $\underset{8}{\underline{}}$. $\underset{4}{\underline{}}$ $\underset{8}{\underline{}}$

$\underset{2}{\underline{}}$ $\underset{6}{\underline{}}$ $\underset{8}{\underline{}}$ $\underset{5}{\underline{}}$ $\underset{3}{\underline{}}$ $\underset{9}{\underline{}}$ $\underset{3}{\underline{}}$ $\underset{4}{\underline{}}$ $\underset{4}{\underline{}}$ $\underset{4}{\underline{}}$ $\underset{8}{\underline{}}$ $\underset{4}{\underline{}}$ $\underset{7}{\underline{}}$ $\underset{3}{\underline{}}$ $\underset{3}{\underline{}}$

$\underset{2}{\underline{}}$ $\underset{6}{\underline{}}$ $\underset{3}{\underline{}}$ $\underset{6}{\underline{}}$ $\underset{6}{\underline{}}$ $\underset{3}{\underline{}}$ - $\underset{4}{\underline{}}$ $\underset{2}{\underline{}}$ $\underset{5}{\underline{}}$ $\underset{3}{\underline{}}$ $\underset{6}{\underline{}}$ $\underset{8}{\underline{}}$ $\underset{6}{\underline{}}$ $\underset{2}{\underline{}}$ $\underset{3}{\underline{}}$ $\underset{7}{\underline{}}$.

1	ABC **2**	DEF **3**
GHI **4**	JKL **5**	MNO **6**
PQRS **7**	TUV **8**	WXYZ **9**
*****	**0**	**#**

Answer on page 64.

BLOOD-SUCKING INSECTS

❋ There are roughly 250 species of blood-sucking lice.

❋ Head lice live on human heads. They hold on to a piece of hair until they are hungry, and then drink blood from the scalp!

❋ Head lice lay eggs, called nits, on their hosts' heads and glue them to hairs with a special substance.

❋ Head lice are light to dark brown in color, not the color of the hair in which they live.

❋ Bird lice live on birds, but they don't drink their blood; instead, they feed on their feathers.

✺ Bedbugs usually bite at night.

✺ Bedbugs can drink up to six times their weight in blood.

🦟 Fleas can jump 100 times their own height.

🦟 There is an audible "click" when a flea jumps.

🦟 Flea larvae don't immediately feed on blood; they eat dead skin, dust, and dirt from their host animal first.

LOVEY-DOVEY

Answer the first clue in each pair with a 5-letter word; answer the second clue on the same line with a 4-letter word. There will be one letter in the first answer that's not used in the second answer. Write this letter in the blank space in the right column. When you have solved the 10 pairs of clues, read *DOWN* to find the nickname for the conenose bug, which likes to bite people's faces and noses. The first line has been done for you.

5-Letter Word	**4-Letter Word**	**Extra Letter**
1. Talk	Small green veggies	
<u>S</u> <u>P</u> <u>E</u> <u>A</u> <u>K</u>	<u>P</u> <u>E</u> <u>A</u> <u>S</u>	<u>K</u>
2. Madrid's country	Cookie, ginger _____	
— — — — —	— — — —	—
3. Opposite of most	Story	
— — — — —	— — — —	—
4. Glide on ice	Grab	
— — — — —	— — — —	—
5. Buckets	Hit hard	
— — — — —	— — — —	—

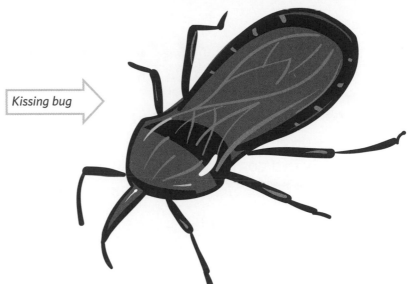

Kissing bug

5-Letter Word	**4-Letter Word**	**Extra Letter**

6. Jet

With less color

— — — — —   — — — —   —

7. Terrific!

Rip

— — — — —   — — — —   —

8. Shaving need, razor _____

Give out the cards

— — — — —   — — — —   —

9. A rodent

A few

— — — — —   — — — —   —

10. Melodies

Male children

— — — — —   — — — —   —

Answer on page 60.

BUTTERFLIES

- Many believe that the butterfly was originally called the "flutterby," but the word comes from the Old English *buttorfleoge*, meaning "milk thief."

- Most butterflies stand on only four of their six legs.

- Butterflies taste with their front legs.

- Butterflies and moths drink nectar through long tongues, which coil up when not being used.

- The color of a butterfly comes from the pigment-bearing scales on its wings.

Monarch butterfly

- Many butterflies have wing patterns visible only in ultraviolet light. Other insects can see them, but humans cannot.

- The scales on butterfly's wings fall off easily when touched; a butterfly can fly without all its scales, but its flight pattern may change.

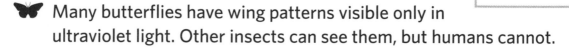

- Some male butterflies drop sweet-scented dust onto females when looking for a mate.

- Male cracker butterflies make cracking sounds by violently flapping their wings to drive away rivals.

- The swallowtail butterfly has the slowest wing beat speed of any insect—300 beats per minute.

Swallowtail butterfly

TAKE A HIKE

Monarch butterflies travel a lot in one day. Solve this puzzle to find out just how fast they can go. Take one letter from the word in COLUMN A to make a new word without changing the order of the letters. Then give that same letter to the word in COLUMN B to make a new word without changing the order of the letters. Write the letter you took and gave in the last column. When you're done, fill in the blanks below to find out the top speed of a butterfly. The first one has been done for you.

	Column A	New Word	Column B	New Word	Letter
1.	THERE	HERE	ILL	TILL	T
2.	SHOCK	————	BAT	————	——
3.	IDEAL	————	TAX	————	——
4.	TRAIL	————	BEAD	————	——
5.	TABLET	————	SEA	————	——
6.	TRYOUT	————	PART	————	——
7.	MOLD	————	CHIP	————	——
8.	NOISE	————	BRAN	————	——
9.	SHOVEL	————	SIPPED	————	——
10.	QUITE	————	MET	————	——
11.	WAIST	————	PEARS	————	——

—— —— —— —— —— ——   —— —— —— —— ——   per hour.

Answer on page 64.

CATERPILLARS

- Caterpillars look as if they have many legs, but they only have six. They are insects after all! Their real legs are near their heads. Other leg-like bumps are muscles called prolegs, which help the caterpillar move.

- Caterpillars have 4,000 muscles, with about 250 of those in their heads. Humans only have 629!

- Caterpillars can increase their body weight thousands of times after only a few weeks of life.

- Some caterpillars are so small that they can tunnel between the upper and lower surfaces of a leaf.

- Some caterpillars are covered in brittle hair that looks soft but breaks off easily. If an enemy tries to swallow the caterpillar, the hair sticks painfully in its mouth, and it spits out the caterpillar.

- Inchworms (also called looper caterpillars) walk by holding on with their front legs and moving up their rear prolegs, then holding on with their prolegs and moving up their front legs.

- Swallowtail butterfly caterpillars have foul-smelling forked glands behind their heads, which they use to hit enemies.

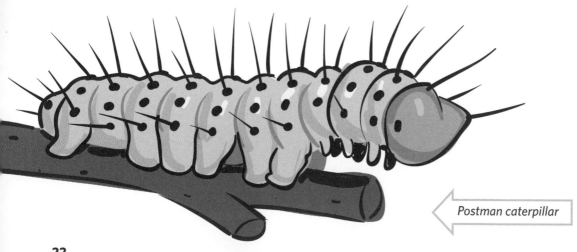

Postman caterpillar

LETHAL DOSE

Postman caterpillars do something weird that makes them deadly to their enemies. To find out what it is, fill in the grid with a word that means the opposite of each word listed to the left of the grid. Then read *DOWN* the starred column for the answer.

1. ALL

2. WHISPER

3. SOUR

4. NEVER

5. ABOVE

6. SHORT

7. OPEN

8. POOR

9. SAD

10. DUMB

11. MAJOR

12. STAND

13. OVER

14. FULL

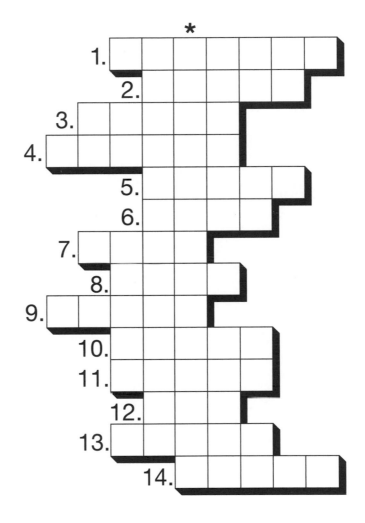

Answer on page 62.

COCKROACHES

🦗 Cockroaches can eat almost anything.

🦗 A cockroach's favorite food is the glue on the back of postage stamps.

🦗 One kind of cockroach lives off body fat when it can't eat or drink. It can live for 90 days without food, or 40 days without food or water!

🦗 Wild cockroaches are less likely to die on their backs than household cockroaches are.

🦗 Household cockroaches carry their eggs in cases attached to their behinds until they hatch.

🦗 Cockroaches and other insects have internal chemical clocks. Even if they are kept in the light for 24 hours, nocturnal insects will only come out at night.

🦗 Female cockroaches can begin to reproduce at about ten weeks old and can produce hundreds of eggs in a lifetime.

🦗 Madagascar hissing cockroaches don't have wings.

🦗 Unlike most insects, which deposit their eggs, Madagascar hissing cockroaches keep their eggs inside their bodies until they hatch.

🦗 A male Madagascar hissing cockroach can tell the difference between a familiar male and a stranger by the sound of its hiss.

COLOR BLIND

The answer to each trivia question is in one of the lines of the grid below. When you find an answer, cross it off, letter by letter. There will always be extra letters on each line. When you've answered all the questions, read the **leftover** letters from *bottom* to *top* and *right* to *left* to find a trivia fact about cockroaches.

1. Bees use the sweet liquid or _____ in flowers to make honey.

2. A _____ is an insect that eats another insect.

3. The silky coverings that moths form around themselves are called _____ .

4. A ____ ____ is a type of wasp.

5. Most insects live together in sections or _____ .

6. The sharp organs of insects that are used to kill or wound prey are known as _____ .

7. Some parts of insects are very strong or _____ .

8. An _____ moth has a large wingspan.

T	H	C	O	C	O	O	N	S	G
N	E	C	T	A	R	I	L	D	E
R	C	A	R	N	I	V	O	R	E
N	I	E	A	T	L	A	S	E	S
T	C	O	L	O	N	I	E	S	O
N	N	H	O	R	N	E	T	A	C
Y	S	T	I	N	G	E	R	S	E
H	P	O	W	E	R	F	U	L	T

Answer on page 60.

CRICKETS

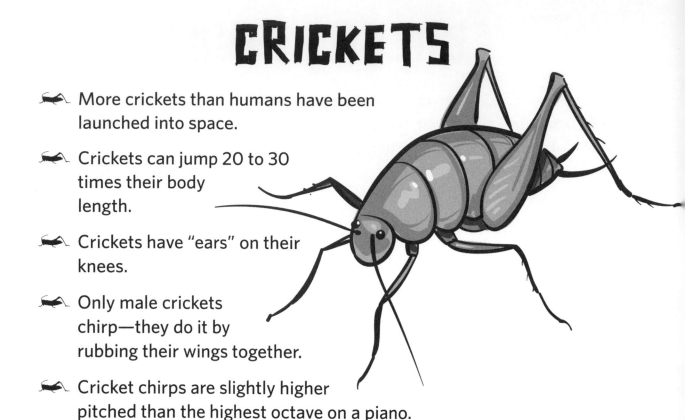

- More crickets than humans have been launched into space.

- Crickets can jump 20 to 30 times their body length.

- Crickets have "ears" on their knees.

- Only male crickets chirp—they do it by rubbing their wings together.

- Cricket chirps are slightly higher pitched than the highest octave on a piano.

- You can find the temperature (in degrees Fahrenheit) by counting the number of times a cricket chirps in 15 seconds and adding 40.

- To convert cricket chirps to degrees Celsius, count the number of chirps in 25 seconds, divide by 3, and then add 4 to get the temperature.

- The ancient Chinese kept crickets as pets, often in elegant golden cages, because their chirping was considered beautiful.

- Mole crickets can't jump, because they don't have the powerful back legs like other crickets; they can only crawl and fly.

- Cave crickets have very long antennae to help them find their way around.

- One species of cricket, the ant cricket, lives only in ant nests.

- Male field crickets attract females by chirping and dancing.

THE "IN" SPORT

An insect-related sport was popular in ancient China. To find the name of this sport, fill in the blank spaces to make words that match the clues (each word contains the letters IN). Then copy the letter on each numbered blank to the same-numbered blank at the bottom of the page.

1. There are 12 of these in a foot

I N __ __ __ __
     1

2. The coldest season

__ I N __ __ __
        12 6

3. Finger jewelry

__ I N __
2   10

4. Husband of a queen

__ I N __
5   15

5. Cake frosting

__ __ I N __
3 4

6. The country next to Pakistan

I N __ __ __
    9

7. The number after 89

__ I N __ __ __
14   7

8. Locate

__ I N __
8

9. Concealing

__ __ __ I N __
11 13

Answer:

__ __ __ __ __ __ __
1 2 3 4 5 6 7

__ __ __ __ __ __ __ __
8 9 10 11 12 13 14 15

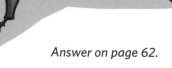

Answer on page 62.

DINNER TIME

- Flower mantises are often brightly colored and have flaps on their bodies resembling flower petals. The mantises wait on flowers to catch unsuspecting prey.

- Some assassin bugs smear their legs with sticky resin that attracts bees; then they attack other insects that come close.

- Ant lions dig pits in sandy soil and wait at the bottom; when prey comes near, they wait for it to slip into the pit or they throw sand at it to make it slip down.

- Geometrid moth caterpillars hold on to branches with their prolegs and stretch their bodies up, disguising themselves as twigs; in this way they both hide from predators and catch and eat unsuspecting insects.

- The praying mantis uses its leaflike appearance to hide from prey. It stands very still and waits until an unsuspecting insect passes by; then the mantis reaches out and grabs it with its powerful front legs.

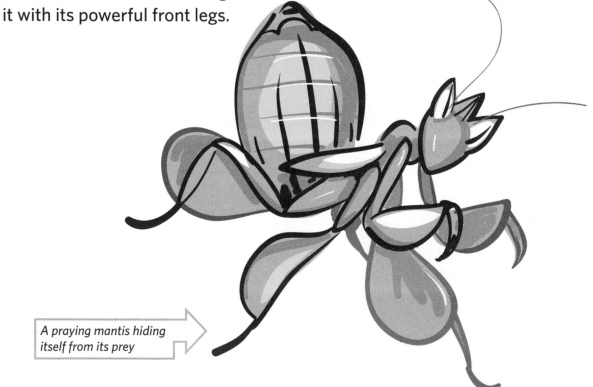

A praying mantis hiding itself from its prey

FLOWER POWER

A certain insect pretends to be a flower so it can eat the insects that try to get nectar from it. To find out the name of this master of disguise, put each flower into the grid in the one spot where it will fit. Then read the **circled** letters from *left* to *right* and *top* to *bottom*. Three letters are already given to get you started.

4 LETTERS
IRIS
LILY
PINK
ROSE

5 LETTERS
ASTER
DAISY
LILAC
POPPY
TULIP

6 LETTERS
AZALEA
CROCUS
MALLOW
VIOLET

7 LETTERS
HEATHER

8 LETTERS
DAFFODIL
HYACINTH
LAVENDER
MAGNOLIA
SNOWDROP
SWEET PEA
TRILLIUM

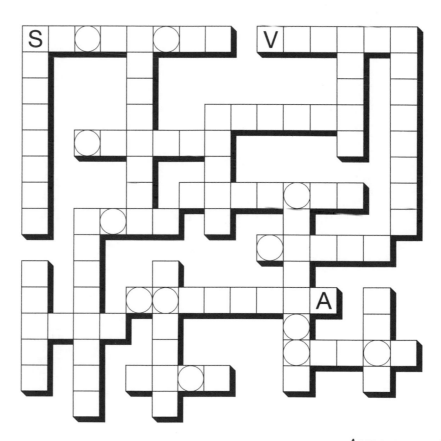

Answer on page 62.

DRAGONFLIES

- Dragonflies have six legs, but they can't walk.

- Dragonflies have two sets of wings, which allow them to hover: One set beats upward while the other beats downward.

- Baby dragonflies (called nymphs) hatch out from eggs in the water. The nymphs don't have wings. They swim before they grow their wings, and they have gills to breathe underwater, like fish.

- Dragonfly nymphs catch small fish and other underwater prey, like mosquito larvae, by shooting out a protruding bottom lip with sharp teeth and pulling in their catch.

- Male dragonflies are extremely territorial and will fight any other male who enters their territory.

- Some dragonflies can fly at more than 30 miles per hour (48 kilometers per hour).

- Dragonflies don't sting—they kill their prey with their legs and jaws.

- Although they don't sting, dragonflies can bite with their powerful jaws if they are threatened.

- Dragonflies' vision responds to ultraviolet light, color, and especially movement.

- Dragonflies can catch and kill prey in midair. They pull their legs into a basket shape as they scoop up prey.

SOME CATCH!

People in Bali eat dragonflies. Sometimes they catch them by hand and other times . . . To finish the sentence, change each letter to the one that comes immediately before it in the alphabet. Write the new words on the lines. Mmm, good!

A B C D E F G H I J K L M N O P Q R S T U V W X Y Z

UIFZ QVU B TUJDLZ

_____

TVCTUBODF PO B MPOH

_____

QPMF BOE UIFO UBQ

_____

B SFTUJOH ESBHPOGMZ,

_____

TUJDLJOH JU UP UIF QPMF.

_____

Answer on page 64.

FLIES

- Some female flies can lay up to 900 eggs at a time.

- Flies' second set of wings have evolved into two knobs called halteres that help them to balance while flying.

- Flies can fly away from any movement they sense in 30 to 50 thousandths of a second.

- Houseflies can land on the ceiling, even though they can't fly upside-down. They fly just below the ceiling, then lift their front legs to grab onto it, and flip their bodies up.

- Flies can walk upside-down or on the sides of walls because they have sticky pads and tiny hairs on their feet.

- When houseflies land on food, they spit saliva all over it to digest it; then they eat it.

- Female horseflies drink animal blood through mouth tubes while pumping saliva into the animal's wound. Male horseflies don't feed on blood at all—they're vegetarians.

- Robber flies feed on other insects by injecting their saliva into the body; this dissolves the prey's insides, which the robber fly sucks out and eats.

- Human warble flies lay eggs on mosquitoes. The mosquitoes transfer the larvae onto the people that the mosquitoes bite, and the larvae bore under the skin to feed for six weeks.

EGGS-ACTLY RIGHT

Bluebottle flies lay their eggs in specific spots. To find out where, put each insect into the grid in alphabetical order. Then read *DOWN* the starred column (ignore the spacing between words when you're writing them in the grid).

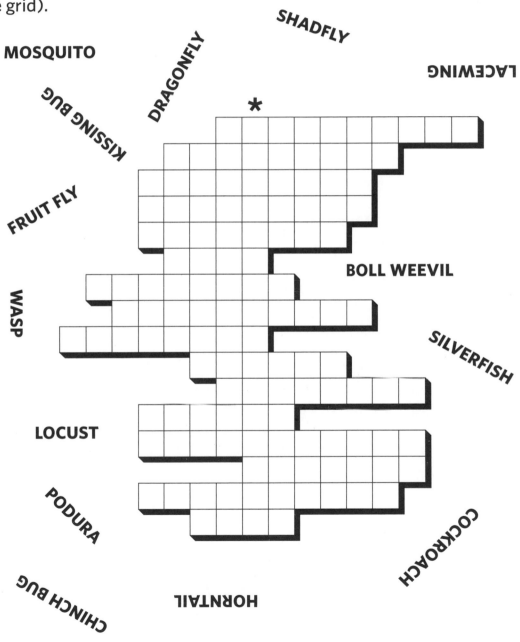

SHADFLY

MOSQUITO

DRAGONFLY

LACEWING

KISSING BUG

*

FRUIT FLY

BOLL WEEVIL

WASP

SILVERFISH

LOCUST

PODURA

COCKROACH

CHINCH BUG

HORNTAIL

Answer on page 62.

GRASSHOPPERS

- For their size, grasshopper muscles are 1,000 times stronger than human muscles. Grasshoppers can jump a distance of 75 to 150 times the length of their bodies.

- Grasshoppers have five eyes: three on the top of their head and one on each side of their head.

- When they are scared, lubber grasshoppers will hiss loudly and produce a foul-smelling froth from their mouths.

- Some grasshoppers can become infested with parasites that infect their brains and make them drown themselves in nearby ponds or streams. The parasite then lives in the water.

- Locusts and grasshoppers are not water-dwellers, but can survive underwater for several minutes without any problems.

- Locusts swarm for food, and their swarms are the largest gatherings of insect life on Earth. They can swarm in gigantic numbers, up to about 10 billion at a time!

- Locusts can fly at almost 10 feet (3 meters) per second. Swarms usually travel from 2 to 6 miles (3.2 to 9.6 kilometers) per day but can cover up to 80 miles per day.

- In Algeria, many people gather large numbers of locusts, cook them in salt water, and dry them in the sun before eating them.

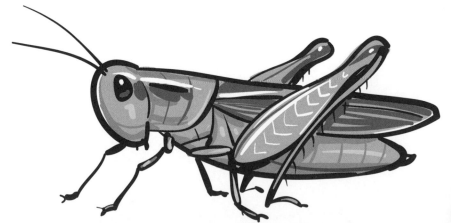

THE INSIDE TRACK

Figure out the letters that are missing on each line and write them in the blanks to form a word that fits the clue. Then take the numbered letters and write them in the same-numbered blanks below to discover something about the insides of grasshoppers.

Something to sit on

C __ __ I R
   2 6

People who serve you in restaurants

W A __ __ __ R S
     11 1 3

Organs of sight

__ __ E S
8 4

Not bad

G O __ __
    16 18

Male parent

F A __ __ E R
    12 5

Not brown hair

__ __ __ N D E
14 15 17

At which place?

__ __ E R E
9 10

At no time

N E __ __ R
    7 13

Answer: __ __ __ __   __ __ __ __
      1 2 3 4   5 6 7 8

__ __ __ __ __   __ __ __ __ __.
9 10 11 12 13 14 15 16 17 18

Answer on page 63.

IS IT SAFE?

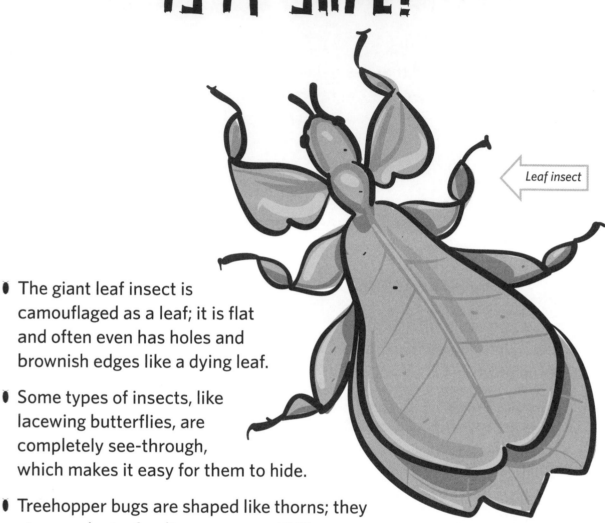

Leaf insect

- The giant leaf insect is camouflaged as a leaf; it is flat and often even has holes and brownish edges like a dying leaf.

- Some types of insects, like lacewing butterflies, are completely see-through, which makes it easy for them to hide.

- Treehopper bugs are shaped like thorns; they stay on plants, feeding on sap, until it's time to move to a new plant. Otherwise, they stay still—like thorns.

- Stick insects not only look like twigs, they move like them! They sway back and forth like twigs being moved in the wind.

- The white underwing moth has dense white hair covering its underside as camouflage.

- Puss moth caterpillars pull their heads into their thoraxes, rear up, and wave whip-like sticks on their backsides to intimidate predators—it makes them look dangerous when they aren't at all.

- Hawk moth caterpillars mimic snakes to keep predators away.

- Some butterflies have large spots on their wings that resemble eyes. This can frighten away potential predators.

- The viceroy butterfly has markings similar to the monarch butterfly, which is poisonous. This tricks enemies into staying away.

- A type of African beetle gathers pollen on its back to disguise itself from predators.

- Some butterflies have different patterns on the tops and bottoms of their wings. This can confuse predators, who look for the open-wing pattern when the butterfly has its wings closed.

- Hoverflies look and fly like bees or wasps, which protects them from being stung or eaten.

- One type of weevil protects itself from predators by acting like a spider.

- Spittlebug nymphs produce piles of frothy bubbles on branches, which they hide in until they become adults.

Stick insect

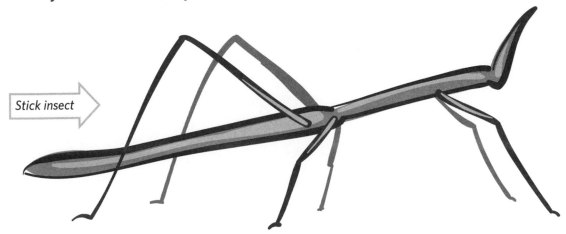

DISGUISE

Inchworms camouflage themselves by pretending to be something else. To find their disguise, follow the directions below, line by line.

1. Write the word INCHWORMS.

_____

2. Get rid of the second vowel.

_____

3. Change the third letter to the one that comes immediately after it in the alphabet.

_____

4. Change the first letter to the first letter of the alphabet.

_____

5. Change the N to the fifth letter of the alphabet.

_____

6. Get rid of the fourth letter.

_____

7. Double the third letter.

_____

8. Put a U before the fifth letter.

_____

9. Change the seventh letter to a J.

_____

10. Change the next to last letter to an H.

_____

11. Move the fourth letter to first place.

_____

12. Switch the second and third letters.

_____

13. Change the fifth, seventh, and eighth letters to the ones that come immediately before them in the alphabet.

_____

14. Put a space between the fourth and fifth letters.

_____

Inchworm

Answer on page 61.

KATYDIDS

- Katydids are close relatives of grasshoppers and crickets.

- Katydids were named for the sound they make, which comes from rubbing their wings together.

- Some species of katydid produce the highest-frequency sound of any insect—too high for humans to hear.

- Most katydids are active at night and have antennae two to three times the lengths of their bodies, which helps them find their way around in the dark.

- A katydid's eardrums are located on its front legs.

- Katydids are not good fliers; they mostly flutter downward and prefer to walk. When katydids land on the ground, they will walk to a nearby tree and climb back up.

- Katydids are prey for many animals and insects, and often hide by mimicking leaves.

- When they are attacked, katydids are able to shed their legs to get away.

- Female katydids have a sharp stinger-like point at the ends of their abdomens, but it isn't actually a stinger—it is an ovipositor, used to deposit the insect's eggs into the ground, in stems of plants, or in tree bark.

HOME SWEET HOME

Half of the 4,000 species of katydids live in one place. Solve this puzzle to name this spot. Each word in the list can become a new word by removing one letter. For example, remove T from CLOSET to get CLOSE. The letter can be removed from anywhere in the word, but the order of the remaining letters will not change. Write the "lost letter" next to each word and then circle the new word in the grid. The words can be horizontal, vertical, or diagonal, and may run forward or backward. When all 19 words have been found, read *DOWN* the column for the answer. The first one has been done for you.

	Word	Lost Letter	New Word
1.	CLOSET	T	CLOSE
2.	SHINGLE	——	————
3.	BEACON	——	————
4.	LAUNCH	——	————
5.	MOTHER	——	————
6.	HURRAY	——	————
7.	PRIZES	——	————
8.	CANOE	——	————
9.	SNACKS	——	————
10.	DRIVERS	——	————
11.	PAINT	——	————
12.	MOVIES	——	————
13.	PRINCE	——	————
14.	FOLDER	——	————
15.	COAST	——	————
16.	STREAM	——	————
17.	FEAST	——	————
18.	SUPPER	——	————
19.	STINGS	——	————

```
P  S  T  E  A  M  Z  U  L  H
R  I  M  U  C  Y  S  D  U  R
I  N  N  Y  P  I  R  R  N  Y
E  G  X  T  N  P  R  T  C  T
S  S  S  G  T  Y  E  P  H  S
A  R  L  Y  F  N  D  R  E  A
C  F  E  W  T  L  L  V  R  C
K  H  G  V  E  S  O  L  C  A
S  T  U  R  I  M  A  Z  M  N
N  O  C  A  B  D  Z  F  T  E
```

Answer on page 63.

LADYBUGS

- Ladybugs are also known as ladybirds or ladybird beetles.

- There are over 4,000 species of ladybug.

- Ladybugs are beetles. They don't just come in red; they can also be orange or yellow.

- Ladybugs' bright color warns enemies that they don't taste good.

- Ladybugs may have zero to 24 spots, depending on the species.

- When ladybugs hatch, some species eat the shell of the egg. The eggs hatch into spiny, black and orange, alligator-like larvae.

- Farmers often use ladybugs to control crop-eating pests. Ladybugs eat aphids and mites, using their small, sharp jaws to turn their prey into a sticky pulp.

- Ladybugs secrete a foul-smelling liquid when they are disturbed. This is called reflex bleeding.

- When they hibernate, ladybugs cluster together.

- Many people consider ladybugs to be good luck.

- Ladybugs may have gotten their name in the Middle Ages, when farmers prayed to the Virgin Mary to save their crops from insect pests. Ladybugs showed up and ate the pests, earning them the name "Beetle of Our Lady."

SOME APPETITE!

Answer each clue and write the letters in the blank spaces. Then move each letter to the same numbered blank in the box below. Work back and forth between the clues and the puzzle box to find a fact about insects with **BIG** appetites. The first one has been done for you.

1. Young boy = $\dfrac{L}{1}\ \dfrac{A}{7}\ \dfrac{D}{38}$

2. Yellow school vehicle = $\dfrac{}{3}\ \dfrac{}{4}\ \dfrac{}{39}$

3. Mommy's husband = $\dfrac{}{2}\ \dfrac{}{35}\ \dfrac{}{13}\ \dfrac{}{36}\ \dfrac{}{11}$

4. Finger jewelry = $\dfrac{}{14}\ \dfrac{}{18}\ \dfrac{}{10}\ \dfrac{}{5}$

5. Purring animal = $\dfrac{}{22}\ \dfrac{}{17}\ \dfrac{}{20}$

6. Sandwich meat = $\dfrac{}{21}\ \dfrac{}{12}\ \dfrac{}{19}$

7. Opposite of in = $\dfrac{}{8}\ \dfrac{}{9}\ \dfrac{}{24}$

8. Opposite of take = $\dfrac{}{15}\ \dfrac{}{28}\ \dfrac{}{6}\ \dfrac{}{30}$

9. Very warm = $\dfrac{}{32}\ \dfrac{}{26}\ \dfrac{}{27}$

10. Cardboard container = $\dfrac{}{25}\ \dfrac{}{33}\ \dfrac{}{29}$

11. Sticky stuff similar to glue = $\dfrac{}{37}\ \dfrac{}{23}\ \dfrac{}{34}\ \dfrac{}{16}\ \dfrac{}{31}$

Answer:

__ A __ Y __ __ __ S   LI __ E   __ B __ __ T
1   2   3 4 5   6   7 8   9

O __ E   __ E __ R .   __ U __ I N __
  10   11   12   13   14   15

__ H __ T T __ __ E   __ __ E Y   __ A N   E __ __
16   17   18 19   20 21   22   23 24

A __ __ U __   S __ __ T __ __ N   T __ __ U __ __ N __
25 26   27   28 29   30 31   32 33   34 35   36

A __ H I __ __ .
37   38 39

Answer on page 64.

43

MOSQUITOES

* A mosquito is actually a type of fly.

* Mosquito eggs float on water and hatch to produce larvae known as wigglers, which live in the water.

* Mosquito larvae cannot breathe underwater. Instead, they stay at the water's surface to take in air.

* Mosquito larvae are eaten by giant water bugs, which helps to control the mosquito population.

* Mosquitoes beat their wings more than 600 times every second.

* The wings of mosquitoes are covered in fringed veins that act like flaps on airplane wings. Under a microscope, their wings look hairy.

* Mosquitoes can smell humans from 20 feet (6 meters) away.

* Mosquitoes sense body heat and carbon dioxide to locate their victims.

* Only female mosquitoes bite.

* Male mosquitoes feed on nectar.

* When they bite animals, mosquitoes inject an anesthetic into the wound so the victim can't feel them sucking the blood.

* Insect repellents such as DEET interfere with the mosquito's ability to smell human sweat.

* Mosquitoes are the number two killer of humans (behind other humans).

* A mosquito can drink up to one-and-a-half times its own weight in blood and still fly away.

IT'S A KILLER

Mosquitoes spread a dangerous disease that kills millions of people all over the world every year. Solve this puzzle to name this deadly disease. The answer to each clue was split into two letter groups and placed in the box below. Take two groups and put them together to form an answer word. Then write the word in the grid going downwards, being sure to match the numbered clue with the same-numbered column. Cross off each letter group as you use it. When all the words are in the grid, read the circled letters from *left* to *right*.

ACH		AFR		FUL		ICA		ING
	IVA		LEA		LOC		PAIN	
PRAY		SAL		STOM		USTS		VES

Clues

1. Abdomen

2. Mouth fluid

3. Grasshoppers

4. Plant parts

5. Begging, like a mantis

6. Large continent

7. Hurting, like an insect bite

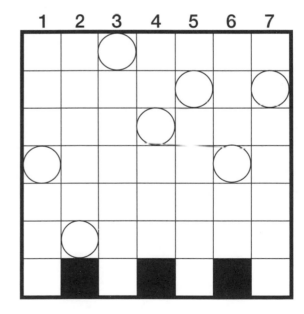

Answer on page 63.

MOTHS

- There are about 160,000 species of moth in the world, but only 17,500 species of butterfly.

- Moths are closely related to butterflies and share many of the same characteristics.

- Moths' bodies are covered in scales, just like butterflies. The scales are made of waste products from the insects' pupal stage.

Luna moth

- Moths shiver to warm up their wings for flight at night.

- Moths rest with their wings unfolded.

- Some moths close their wings and drop to the ground when they sense a bat nearby.

- Some moths have ears on their wings.

- A female moth's scent can be picked up by a male almost 7 miles (11 km) away.

- Atlas moths have a greater wing area than any other insect, with wingspans of more than 11 inches (28 cm).

- The female vaporer moth has no wings. It lives in its pupa and waits for a male to find it; then it lays eggs and dies.

- Hawk moths beat their wings about 5,400 times per minute.

- The Madagascar hawk moth has a tongue between 12 and 14 inches (30 and 36 cm) long—several times the length of its body.

- Tiger moths make a high-pitched clicking noise to warn away predators.

- Some adult moths do not feed because they don't have mouth parts.

FLIGHT PLAN

Insects travel at different times of the day. Solve this puzzle to find one insect's regular flight plan. Each word in the list can become a new word by adding one letter. For example, add M to SELL to get SMELL. The letter can be added anywhere in the word, but the order of the remaining letters will not change. Write the "found letter" next to each word, and then find and circle the new word in the grid. The words can be horizontal, vertical, or diagonal, and may run forward or backward. When all 19 words have been found, read *DOWN* the column of found letters for the answer. The first one has been done for you.

Word	Found Letter	New Word
1. SELL	__M__	__SMELL__
2. SHUT	___	_____
3. EXIT	___	_____
4. SAYING	___	_____
5. ASKS	___	_____
6. CARTON	___	_____
7. DARED	___	_____
8. SIPPING	___	_____
9. WORD	___	_____
10. LIPS	___	_____
11. BEACH	___	_____
12. EAST	___	_____
13. HORSE	___	_____
14. PAIN	___	_____
15. SORE	___	_____
16. MAZE	___	_____
17. LANDS	___	_____
18. TANKS	___	_____
19. HERE	___	_____

```
Y  S  G  N  I  Y  A  T  S  S
B  H  D  R  A  E  W  H  M  H
C  I  E  X  I  S  T  E  A  O
A  P  T  Y  B  G  L  R  S  U
R  P  R  H  E  L  Z  E  K  T
T  I  A  Y  A  A  E  N  S  X
O  N  D  V  D  N  S  A  Z  S
O  G  I  R  M  D  K  T  C  O
N  H  O  A  R  S  E  S  R  H
A  W  N  S  P  I  L  F  Y  R
S  N  O  R  E  Z  I  A  M  W
```

Answer on page 61.

PRAYING MANTISES

- Praying mantises are carnivores—they eat other insects and sometimes they are cannibals.

- A praying mantis captures its prey by pinning it between its two front legs.

- Most of the time, praying mantises will wait quietly for prey to come close, but they sometimes stalk their prey.

- Praying mantises are the only insects that feed on moths at night and that are fast enough to catch flies and mosquitoes.

- Mantises sometimes attack and eat small frogs and birds.

- Praying mantises don't bite, but their spiny forelegs are sharp and can be painful to touch.

- Male praying mantises are smaller than females.

- Female praying mantises often bite off their mates' heads and eat their bodies during mating.

- The praying mantis can move its head from side to side (180°). It is the only insect that can do this.

- Praying mantises' binocular vision allows them to tell how far away their prey is.

- Females praying mantises lay their eggs in frothy substances attached to trees, plants, or other objects.

- Cockroaches, crickets, and grasshoppers are the closest insect relatives of praying mantises.

RAW DEAL

Answer each clue and write the letters in the blank spaces. Then copy each letter to the same-numbered blank in the answer lines below. Work back and forth, and when all the letters have been filled in, read from 1 to 41 to discover how hungry praying mantises really are.

1. Evening

    __ __ __ __ __
    37 32 7 16 1

2. Half of ten

    __ __ __ __
    26 30 35 3

3. Word that follows "Scotch" or "masking"

    __ __ __ __
    15 40 20 25

4. A mean dog might do this

    __ __ __ __
    24 8 10 17

5. Finished

    __ __ __ __
    41 27 9 22

6. "My country, tis of ____"

    __ __ __ __
    31 2 36 12

7. Filthy

    __ __ __ __ __
    38 18 28 14 4

8. Wear this after a bath

    __ __ __ __
    21 11 5 39

9. Use your eyes

    __ __ __
    33 29 34

10. Twelve months = one ____

    __ __ __ __
    23 6 13 19

Answer:

__ __ __ __   __ __ __ __ __   __ __
1 2 3 4   5 6 7 8 9   10 11

__ __ __   __ __ __ __ __   __ __ __ __
12 13 14   15 16 17 18 19   20 21 22 23

__ __ __ __ __ __   __ __   __ __
24 25 26 27 28 29   30 31   32 33

__ __ __ __   __ __ __ __ .
34 35 36 37   38 39 40 41

Answer on page 63.

TERMITES

- Termites are social insects that live in colonies. The colonies may have as many as several million termites!

- Termite colonies have both a king and a queen, unlike other insect colonies, which only have queens.

- Termite queens live for 15 to 25 years and lay an egg every few seconds for most of their lives.

- Termite queens bloat into huge, immobile lumps while producing eggs. They rely completely on worker termites to care for them. The worker termites are blind.

- Termite mounds (or termitaries) are the tallest insect structures, sometimes as tall as 20 feet (7.5 meters)!

- Termite mounds have great air circulation: Hot air is sucked out of the nest and replaced with cool air from outside. The termites control the air flow by changing the size of the tunnels.

- Termite mounds have narrow walls that always point directly north and south.

- Termites and ants are enemies. Ants often raid termite nests to eat the workers and young.

- Some termites fight enemies by shooting sticky goo from their mouths, using their abdominal muscles. Sometimes this causes so much pressure that the insect's whole body explodes.

- Termite species in many parts of the world build ball-shaped nests from dirt, chewed-up wood, and their own saliva.

- In Africa, termites build nests with mushroom-shaped tops to protect themselves from the rain.

- Termites prefer to eat dead leaves and wood over green, living plants. In their nests, fungus in rotting wood supplies them with nitrogen, vitamins, and other nutrients.

- Over time, termites cause a lot of damage to wooden structures, such as houses, by feeding on them.

WOOD YOU?

Solve this puzzle to discover exactly what termites feast on. Find and circle the fourteen types of wood in the list. Look up, down, and diagonally both forward and backward. Then take the **leftover** letters from the grid and read them from *left* to *right* and *top* to *bottom* to finish this sentence: Termites eat. . .

ASH

BAMBOO

BIRCH

CEDAR

CHERRY

CYPRESS

ELM

HAZEL

HICKORY

MAHOGANY

MAPLE

SYCAMORE

TEAK

WALNUT

S	T	O	O	B	M	A	B	H
Y	Y	R	O	K	C	I	H	A
R	N	C	Y	P	R	E	S	S
R	A	E	A	C	L	S	O	H
E	G	D	H	M	F	T	P	A
H	O	A	E	R	O	T	K	Z
C	H	S	O	C	F	R	A	E
M	A	P	L	E	W	O	E	L
O	M	W	A	L	N	U	T	D

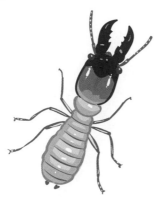

Answer on page 61.

TRUE BUGS

- Most people think "bug" is just another name for insect. Actually, true bugs are a specific group of insects: the Hemiptera.

- True bugs make up about 8% of insect species.

- True bugs—such as aphids, stinkbugs, and cicadas—have long feeding tubes for piercing and sucking.

- When aphids drink plant sap, they drink so much that is shoots out the back of them as honeydew, which ants eat.

- Not all aphids lay eggs—some can have live young without mating at all!

- A female aphid can have about 50 baby aphids in a week—**every** week!

- Aphids can begin to bear young six to eight days after being born.

- Giant water bugs catch prey such as frogs and fish underwater with their powerful front legs.

- Backswimmers are water bugs that live upside-down below the surface of the water, catching prey that lands on the surface.

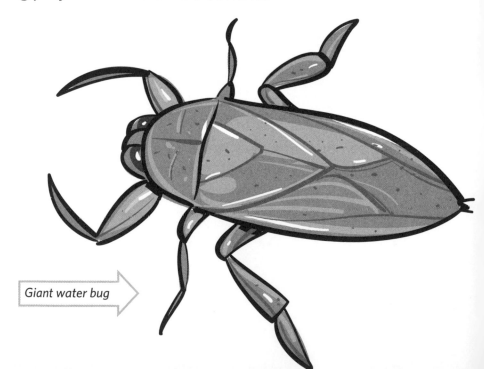

Giant water bug

ALIAS

To learn another name for the water strider, an insect with tiny water-repellent hairs on its legs that allow it to walk on water, place the name of each body of water listed at left into the grid. Use the letters that are already in the grid, as well as the number of letters in each word or phrase, to guide you. When the grid is filled in, read *DOWN* the starred column to find the two-word name.

1. **BROOK**

2. **CHANNEL**

3. **CREEK**

4. **LAKE**

5. **OCEAN**

6. **POOL**

7. **SEA**

8. **SOUND**

9. **STRAIT**

10. **STREAM**

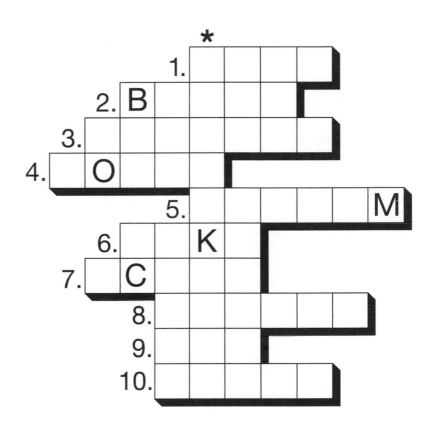

Answer on page 63.

MORE BUGS

- Male giant water bugs carry batches of eggs glued to their backs until they hatch.

- Assassin bugs ambush other insects; then they kill them and eat them.

- Water scorpions breathe through a long snorkel-like tube in their backsides.

- Aphids produce and release an alarm chemical called a pheromone, which alerts other aphids of a predator's presence.

- Aphids are sometimes protected and controlled by farmer ants that "milk" them for their honeydew.

- The honeydew that aphids produce could build up and kill them if ants didn't eat it first.

- A male cicada can buzz at 100 decibels, loud enough for its mating call to be heard up to a mile (1.6 kilometers) away.

- Some tropical cicadas can measure 6 inches (15 centimeters)—as long as an adult human hand.

Cicada

HIDING OUT

Twenty-one words (or parts of words) were removed from the paragraph below. Reconstruct the sentences by taking each word from the box and putting it into its correct position in the paragraph. Do it correctly and you'll find an interesting bug fact. Cross off each word as you use it, because it will only fit into one spot. Hint: Everything must make sense!

AD	AFTER	AN	EAR	EVENT	FEE	HE
HEIR	HEY	LOW	ME	ON	OR	RAT
ROOT	ROUND	SEE	SEVEN	SO	SHORT	WON

_____ME CIC_____AS HIDE OUT F_____ L_____G

PERIODS OF TI_____. THEY _____D ON TREE _____S AND

LIVE BE_____ G_____ FOR S_____EEN Y_____S.

T_____ COME OUT OF T_____ GROUND AS ADULTS, LAY

T_____ EGGS, _____D DIE _____LY _____WARDS.

THE NEXT GENE_____ION _____'T BE _____N FOR

_____TEEN YEARS.

Answer on page 61.

WASPS

✳ There are about 20,000 species of wasp.

✳ To make sure their stingers stay lodged in prey long enough to inject poison, wasp stingers have jagged edges.

✳ Wasps use their stingers to kill or paralyze their prey, while solitary bees sting only in self-defense.

✳ Wasps are very important in pest control: Almost every species of pest has a wasp species that preys upon it.

✳ Queen common wasps begin to build new hives by themselves, chewing up wood to build walls around their eggs. When the eggs hatch, the new wasps help to finish the nest.

✳ Female hunting wasps inject their prey with a poison that paralyzes them. Then they lay an egg on it, bury them both, and leave their prey as food for their newly hatched young.

✳ Parasitic wasps deposit their eggs in or on other insects. When the eggs hatch, the larvae eat the host from the inside out.

✳ Some wasps lay their eggs inside other insects' eggs. The wasps hatch first and eat the other insect's young.

✳ Mymarid wasps are the smallest insects— about 0.007 inch (0.18 millimeter).

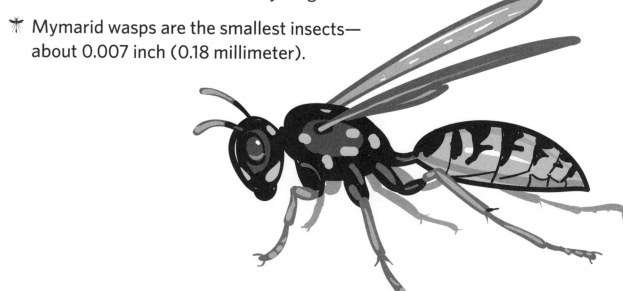

BABY BOOM

Do you know how many baby wasps are born in one season? To find out, change each letter below to the letter that comes immediately *before* or *after* it in the alphabet. Example: B can be changed to A or C. Choose the correct letter and your bug-ability will skyrocket!

A B C D E F G H I J K L M N O P Q R S T U V W X Y Z

B PTFDO VBTQ BBO

_____

IBUF BANTS GHUD

_____

UINVRBMC NGETQSHOF

_____

JO B RHMFMF TTNLDS.

_____

Answer on page 63.

WHAT'S LEFT?

- Stick insects can reproduce without mating. They are popular pets, especially the larger species.

- Some giant stick insects can grow to about 12 inches (30 centimeters) long.

- Earwigs don't have ears, but their feet are very sensitive to motion.

- Earwig mothers are among the few insects that raise their young. They tend to the eggs until they hatch, licking them to remove mold, and then stay with their young for several months.

- Earwigs use their rear pincers in self-defense and to capture prey.

- Silverfish are very primitive insects; they have changed very little since they first appeared more than 350 million years ago.

- Silverfish hide in houses during the day and come out at night to feed on algae, lichens, and starchy food.

- Phantom midges are almost transparent in the larval stage. When they swarm together, they look like clouds of smoke.

- Stylopids are strange parasitic insects. The females live inside the abdomens of bees and wasps with a small part of their body sticking out. The males mate with the part that is sticking out and the female insect's larvae then drop onto flowers and find new hosts.

- Sea skaters are the only insects that live on the open sea.

- Springtails are tiny, wingless insects that leap high into the air by folding their tails under their bodies and then releasing them like a spring.

Silverfish

MYTH STAKES

Answer each clue and write the answer's letters in the blank spaces at the clue's right. Then copy each letter to the same-numbered blank in the answer sentence below. Work back and forth, and when all the letters have been filled in, read from 1 to 40 to find a myth that people once believed about earwigs and how they kill people.

1. Opposite of no

—— —— ——
4 16 22

2. Game, _____ and seek

—— —— —— ——
2 17 25 19

3. It travels on a track

—— —— —— —— ——
12 6 20 34 11

4. Dirt, used for potting plants

—— —— —— ——
36 13 32 9

5. Time of year when it snows

—— —— —— —— —— ——
8 10 24 14 3 18

6. Opposite of loved

—— —— —— —— ——
15 7 29 26 38

7. To frighten

—— —— —— —— ——
40 5 27 33 39

8. A soft metal used in cans

—— —— ——
28 37 35

9. Symbol of Valentine's Day

—— —— —— —— ——
30 31 23 21 1

Answer:

—— —— —— ——   —— —— —— —— ——   —— —— —— ——
1 2 3 4   5 6 7 8 9   10 11 12 13

—— —— —— —— ——   —— —— —— ——   —— —— ——
14 15 16 17 18   19 20 21 22   23 24 25

—— —— ——   —— —— —— —— ——
26 27 28   29 30 31 32 33

—— —— —— —— —— —— —— .
34 35 36 37 38 39 40

Answer on page 61.

ANSWERS

SPICE IT UP
page 5

```
P E A T I M U S T A R D D
N E C I R O C I L Y E E
D G P G A R F L E R G E
O I I P C A T L M A A S
L T L I E G S L S M R X
I H N L T R K A A E O A
S E Y E A E M N E S B L
A A P M L I N O S R F
B E C T S I A S N R W A
C H I V E S P E Y T F R
O M Y O S H A L L O T U
```

Answer: **Eating garlic might keep insects away from you.**

HOUSING ARRANGEMENTS
pages 10–11

1. HU**M**AN
   GR**O**UP
   WA**S**TE
   WA**T**CH

2. HO**B**BY
   SW**E**AT
   CH**E**SS
   ME**S**SY

3. SO**L**ID
   CR**I**SP
   SE**V**EN
   QU**EE**N

4. BO**A**RD
   HE**LL**O
   CL**O**WN
   SI**N**CE
   BR**E**AK

5. PU**N**CH
   SP**OO**N
   FE**T**CH

6. BR**I**SK
   RA**N**CH

7. OC**C**UR
   ST**O**NE
   SI**LL**Y
   CR**O**WD
   WI**N**GS
   GR**I**ME
   BL**EE**D
   PA**S**TE

Answer: **Most bees live alone, not in colonies.**

LOVEY-DOVEY
pages 18–19

1.	SPEAK	PEAS	**K**
2.	SPAIN	SNAP	**I**
3.	LEAST	TALE	**S**
4.	SKATE	TAKE	**S**
5.	PAILS	SLAP	**I**
6.	PLANE	PALE	**N**
7.	GREAT	TEAR	**G**
8.	BLADE	DEAL	**B**
9.	MOUSE	SOME	**U**
10.	SONGS	SONS	**G**

Answer: **Kissing bug**

COLOR BLIND
page 25

1. Nectar
2. Carnivore
3. Cocoons
4. Hornet
5. Colonies
6. Stingers
7. Powerful
8. Atlas

Answer: **They cannot see in red light.**

MYTH STAKES

page 59

1. Yes
2. Hide
3. Train
4. Soil
5. Winter
6. Hated
7. Scare
8. Tin
9. Heart

Answer: **They crawl into their ears and eat their insides.**

WOOD YOU?

page 51

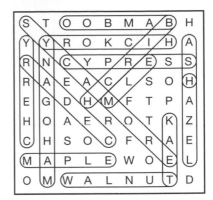

Answer: **. . . the soft parts of wood.**

FLIGHT PLAN

page 47

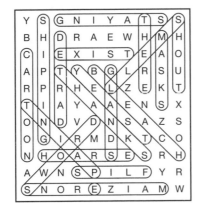

1. Sell/Smell
2. Shut/Shout
3. Exit/Exist
4. Saying/Staying
5. Asks/Masks
6. Carton/Cartoon
7. Dared/Darted
8. Sipping/Shipping
9. Word/Sword
10. Lips/Flips
11. Beach/Bleach
12. East/Yeast
13. Horse/Hoarse
14. Pain/Paint
15. Sore/Snore
16. Maze/Maize
17. Lands/Glands
18. Tanks/Thanks
19. Here/There

Answer: **Most moths fly at night.**

HIDING OUT

page 55

SOME CICAD**AS** HIDE OUT **FOR LON**G PERIODS OF TI**ME**. THEY **FEE**D ON TREE **ROOT**S AND LIVE BE**LOW GROUND** FOR S**EVENT**EEN Y**EAR**S. T**HEY** COME OUT OF T**HE** GROUND AS ADULTS, LAY T**HEIR** EGGS, **AN**D DIE **SHORT**LY **AFTER**WARDS. THE NEXT GENE**RAT**ION **WON**'T BE **SEE**N FOR **SEVEN**TEEN YEARS.

DISGUISE

pages 38–39

1. INCHWORMS
2. INCHWRMS
3. INDHWRMS
4. ANDHWRMS
5. AEDHWRMS
6. AEDWRMS
7. AEDDWRMS
8. AEDDUWRMS
9. AEDDUWJMS
10. AEDDUWJHS
11. DAEDUWJHS
12. DEADUWJHS
13. DEADTWIGS
14. DEAD TWIGS

BRRR!

page 9

```
MAYBE   REASON
A       I    HE
RAINING G    HE
B V     HANDLE
BLOOSE  T    EXACTLY
E R      IDEA C
  Y                T
  YEAR             L
  X                Y
S INSPECT
KNOT    O A
A    E  U N
I    Y  N D
LIKE    DRYING
```

Answer: **Midges and lice**

EYE SEE YOU

page 13

1. ANOT**HER**
2. EL**AST**IC
3. IN**TELL**IGENT
4. T**WIN**KLE
5. BE**LONG**INGS
6. **HIGH**WAY
7. **BREAK**FAST
8. WINDM**ILL**
9. F**EAST**ING

Answer: **Whirligig beetle**

LETHAL DOSE

page 23

1. NOTHING
2. SHOUT
3. SWEET
4. ALWAYS
5. BELOW
6. TALL
7. SHUT
8. RICH
9. HAPPY
10. SMART
11. MINOR
12. SIT
13. UNDER
14. EMPTY

Answer: **They eat cyanide**

THE "IN" SPORT

page 27

1. INCHES
2. WINTER
3. RING
4. KING
5. ICING
6. INDIA
7. NINETY
8. FIND
9. HIDING

Answer: **Cricket fighting**

FLOWER POWER

page 29

Answer: **Orchid mantis** (it disguises itself as an orchid blossom)

EGGS-ACTLY RIGHT

page 33

```
BOLLWEEVIL
CHINCHBUG
COCKROACH
DRAGONFLY
FRUITFLY
GNAT
HORNTAIL
KISSINGBUG
LACEWING
LOCUST
MOSQUITO
PODURA
SCORPIONFLY
SHADFLY
SILVERFISH
WASP
```

Answer: **On rotting corpses**

THE INSIDE TRACK

page 35

CHAIR
WA**ITE**RS
EYES
GO**OD**
FA**TH**ER
BLONDE
WHERE
NE**VE**R

Answer: **They have white blood.**

HOME SWEET HOME

page 41

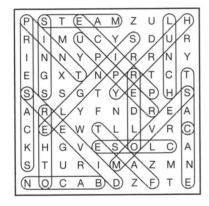

1. Closet/Close
2. Shingle/Single
3. Beacon/Bacon
4. Launch/Lunch
5. Mother/Other
6. Hurray/Hurry
7. Prizes/Pries
8. Canoe/Cane
9. Snacks/Sacks
10. Drivers/Divers
11. Paint/Pint
12. Movies/Moves
13. Prince/Price
14. Folder/Older
15. Coast/Cast
16. Stream/Steam
17. Feast/Fast
18. Supper/Upper
19. Stings/Sings

Answer: **The Amazon rain forest**

IT'S A KILLER

page 45

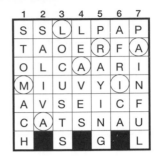

Answer: **Malaria**

RAW DEAL

page 49

1. Night
2. Five
3. Tape
4. Bite
5. Done
6. Thee
7. Dirty
8. Robe
9. See
10. Year

Answer: **They begin to eat their prey before it is even dead.**

ALIAS

page 53

Answer: **Pond Skater**

BABY BOOM

page 57

Answer: **A queen wasp can have about five thousand offspring in a single summer.**

SEW WHAT?
page 7

1. FIRE **WOOD** CHUCK
2. SWEET **HEART** ACHE
3. PINE **APPLE** SAUCE
4. PUPPY **LOVE** LETTER
5. NAVY **BLUE** BERRY
6. FOR **EVER** GREEN
7. COFFEE **TABLE** CLOTH
8. BRAND **NEW** ENGLAND
9. FLASH **LIGHT** HOUSE
10. OUT **SIDE** WALK

Answer: **Weaver ants**

BIG DEAL
page 15

Answer: **The Goliath beetle is the heaviest insect. It could weigh three and one-half ounces.**

TAKE A HIKE
page 21

	Column A	New Word	Column B	New Word	Letter
1.	THERE	**HERE**	ILL	**TILL**	T
2.	SHOCK	**SOCK**	BAT	**BATH**	H
3.	IDEAL	**DEAL**	TAX	**TAXI**	I
4.	TRAIL	**TAIL**	BEAD	**BREAD**	R
5.	TABLET	**TABLE**	SEA	**SEAT**	T
6.	TRYOUT	**TROUT**	PART	**PARTY**	Y
7.	MOLD	**OLD**	CHIP	**CHIMP**	M
8.	NOISE	**NOSE**	BRAN	**BRAIN**	I
9.	SHOVEL	**SHOVE**	SIPPED	**SLIPPED**	L
10.	QUITE	**QUIT**	MET	**MEET**	E
11.	WAIST	**WAIT**	PEARS	**SPEARS**	S

Answer: **Thirty miles per hour**

SOME CATCH!
page 31

Answer: **They put a sticky substance on a long pole and then tap a resting dragonfly, sticking it to the pole.**

SOME APPETITE!
page 43

1. LAD
2. BUS
3. DADDY
4. RING
5. CAT
6. HAM
7. OUT
8. GIVE
9. HOT
10. BOX
11. PASTE

Answer: **Ladybugs live about one year. During that time they can eat about sixteen thousand aphids.**